Words of Comfort

Words of Comfort

What to Say at Times of Sadness or Loss

William John Fitzgerald

ACTA
ASSISTING CHRISTIANS TO ACT
PUBLICATIONS

Words of Comfort
What to Say at Times of Sadness or Loss
by William John Fitzgerald

Edited by Kass Dotterweich
Cover Design by Tom A. Wright
Typesetting by Garrison Publications

Published by ACTA Publications
            Assisting Christians To Act
            4848 N. Clark Street
            Chicago, IL 60640
            800-397-2282

Library of Congress Catalog number: 98-74565

ISBN: 0-87946-196-9

Printed in the United States of America

03 02 01 00 99 5 4 3 2 1 First Printing

CONTENTS

PART 2: LOSSES THROUGH DEATH

DEDICATION

To all ministers of consolation,
including
Joan Houtekier, Joyce Rupp, Val Peter,
Bishop Anthony Milone,
Ron and Duffi Goodrich,
and Eugene Maguire,
with special appreciation to
William Healy,
Peggy Deegan and Adrienne Smith.

How to Use This Book

When friends and loved ones experience the pain of loss and grief, you might not know exactly what to say—or what to pray. This book is a resource that provides some words you may be searching for. It can be used in a variety of ways:

- Let the images, Scripture passages, and prayers contained here for each specific occasion inspire your own imagination. Try writing a personal note that incorporates in your own words one or more of the ideas that come to you. Don't be afraid that they are not "deep" or "literary" enough. Your effort to write something special is what will be appreciated and remembered. (If you are creating your own card, you might want to draw or import on your computer an icon or piece of clip art that brings the suggested image to mind.)

- If a particular phrase or image or indeed an entire selection from this book strikes you as just what you want to say, use it. You need not secure permission from the publisher or author to use this material in a personal letter or note—this is exactly what the book was designed for! Write as if the thoughts and phrasing were your own (or if you don't feel comfortable with that, say something like "I read this in a book and feel it says exactly what I want to say").

- If you like a particular prayer, you can use it every day and assure those experiencing the sadness or loss that you are saying a special prayer for them. Or, if you think it would bring them comfort, you can incorporate all or part of the prayer into your personal note. (The same can be done with the Scripture passages.)

- Obviously, anytime you use any words of comfort from this book you should personalize it as much as possible. Instead of saying "my friend" or "my loved one," for example, you should use the person's name. Likewise, if the situation is slightly different from the one in the book, you should change what you say accordingly to be as specific as possible.

Whatever you write, you should draft your comfort note with sensitivity. Remember that it is not possible for you to rescue someone from the pain of sadness or loss. Rather, effective words of comfort validate a person's pain, convey support and love, and offer solidarity during a difficult time. Statements such as "I know just how you feel" or "Next month things will be better" or even "This is God's will" are usually inappropriate.

Here are some of the elements of a personal note that you might want to consider:

1. Express solidarity with the other person. For example, you might want to open with something like "I want you to know that you are in my thoughts and prayers in your time of sorrow" or "I was so saddened when I heard about your loss."

2. Show that you are aware of the other's feelings, without trying to diminish the pain or confusion or offering a way to fix the

situation. For example, if a person is getting a divorce or has just ended a relationship you might say, "I'm sure you are lonely at times," without adding, "so maybe you should start dating as soon as possible."

3. Offer an image or bit of poetry or Scripture (from this book or others) that might offer comfort or solace. For example, if your friend or loved one has lost an infant, you might write something like this from page 96:

    > Like children who led the Lord
    > on the Sunday of palms,
    > holy innocents go before,
    > wait for us at heaven's door.

4. Promise that you will say a special prayer for the person or, if you like, include the prayer in your comfort note. For example, you could say, "I found this prayer in a book, and I thought I would share it with you. This will be my prayer for you during this time of sadness."

5. You can end by offering to help in any way. For example, you might say, "Let me know if there is anything I can do, even if you just need someone to listen or a shoulder to cry on."

We can often touch the sorrow of others and offer them a soothing balm of genuine love by simply sending them a few words of comfort. This book is an attempt to suggest some words that you might use, but it is not the words that ultimately matter to the person experiencing sadness or loss. It is your care, consideration, compassion and thoughtfulness—all of which are genuinely and completely yours.

Part 1:
Losses throughout Life

The Lord is my shepherd,
I shall not want.

Psalm 23:1

Divorce

IMAGE: WALKING ON WATER

Like the exuberant Peter stepping out of the boat onto the surface of the Sea of Galilee, most of us spent our youth believing we could walk on water. We believed that our major life decisions would somehow be supported by the world around us. Many of us dreamed of marriage to a beloved life partner with whom we would grow old.

But life doesn't always remain steady and predictable. Storms brew, dark clouds appear at the edge of the horizon, and winds lash. Calm seas begin to roll and foam, and hands stretched out in hope simply do not find a grip.

Friends need to stand by when marriages run aground—if only to say, "We are with you. You can count on us."

Scripture

Peter answered him, "Lord, if it is you, command me to come to you on the water." He said, "Come." So Peter got out of the boat, started walking on the water, and came toward Jesus. But when he noticed the strong wind, he became frightened, and beginning to sink, he cried out, "Lord, save me!"

Matthew 14:28-30

Prayer

You helped your disciples overcome their fear during the storm at sea, Lord. Reach out your hand to my dear ones who suffer from the storms of divorce. Calm the seething waters that toss them around. Let a beacon of hope flicker beyond their present pain. Help them in their search for a safe harbor where life can begin again.

Moving Far Away

IMAGE: WILD GEESE FLYING IN FORMATION

For the wild geese, being "in place" during the long seasonal migrations means being on the wing, smoothing the way for one another into oncoming winds. Their jour-neys take them toward the hospitable northlands in summer and back again to warm and inviting southlands in winter.

Each spring and fall, the wild geese cut a flight path far above human caravans also on the move: families and individuals relo-cating as they respond to job opportunities or simply seek more hospitable environ-ments. We humans can learn from the geese. We, too, can smooth the moving paths for one another and ease the pain of separa-tion from family members and neighbors by pledging a loyalty that will span the dis-tance.

Scripture

"Where you go, I will go;
  Where you lodge, I will lodge;
your people shall be my people,
and your God my God."

Ruth 1:16

Prayer

Jesus, your earliest experience of child-hood was a move from Galilee to Egypt and back again. Please bless this jour-ney of moving for my friends. May your holy angels soar over their moving path and be guides to a new home in a dis-tant place.

With the angels, I send my loyalty and love as their companions. For the hearts of those who love are never really sepa-rated; they are only stretched by time and space.

The End of a Loving Relationship

IMAGE: THE CHANGING SEASONS

All the seasons have certain characteristics that we particularly enjoy. Usually, however, we like one or two seasons more than the others.

Our preference for any given season, however, does not influence the inevitable change of one season moving on for the early realities of the season coming in behind it. The warm and gentle days of summer will give way to a brisk and colorful autumn, which in turn will change to winter. Inevitably, the grass will, once again, be a rich spring green as those warm and gentle days of summer return.

The loss of a loving relationship is like that, for life is about change. As much as we love and enjoy our relationships with others, time brings change—and the change is often painful. Given time to heal, however, we can be stronger and wiser for having loved.

Scripture

For everything there is a season, and a
time for every matter under heaven:
...a time to break down, and a time to
    build up;
a time to weep, and a time to laugh;
a time to mourn, and a time to dance;
a time to throw away stones, and a time
    to gather stones together;
a time to embrace, and a time to refrain
    from embracing;
a time to seek, and a time to lose.

Ecclesiastes 3:1, 3-6

Prayer

O God, this is a time to grieve and a
season to seek. The loss of love leaves a
deep chasm to be mourned and a wound
to be healed for my good friend. Send
your healing now to embrace this heart
that hurts for having loved.

One day at a time, through prayer, may
a circle of love form around this
wounded heart, a circle that proclaims:
"You are not alone, for those who care
stand with you in a holy circle, both in
the best of times and in the worst of
times."

The Empty Nest

IMAGE: A TEN-SPEED MOUNTAIN BIKE

We might imagine the first half of life to be like riding a ten-speed mountain bike up hills, through valleys—full speed ahead. We hold tightly to the handlebars and take control of the terrain, going where we want to go. We manage our household, our family, our finances, our careers. Confidently, we brave the wind and use all ten speeds to keep moving, to get where we want to go.

The second half of life is a slowing-down process. We're still on the bike, but the path narrows. It's time for slowing down and letting go. As the last child leaves home, time takes on a different meaning as gears shift to a slower pace. There is time to look about, to gaze lovingly, to see more, and to develop the unexplored pathways that freedom brings. There is time to grow in new and exciting ways.

Scripture

May our sons in their youth
be like plants full grown,
our daughters like corner pillars,
cut for the building of a palace.
Psalm 144:12

Prayer

Life is not less for my friends, O God; it
is only different. The pace has changed.
Time offers a new meaning. Open their
hearts to see that, yes, this is a bitter-
sweet moment—but one that promises
so much. Lend your speed to their family
and guide their pathways.

Retirement

IMAGE: REPLACING A FLAT TIRE

The immediate feeling that often accompanies retirement might be like the experience of having a flat tire. After zooming along the road of life and work at a routine and familiar pace, the arrival of retirement sometimes creates the feeling of a sudden stop. Flat! Deflated!

The challenge is to dig out the spare, put it in place, and get going again. In retirement this might be an old hobby revisited, a new hobby often pondered, an opportunity to volunteer for a favorite cause, the chance to study and learn new and exciting skills. The retirement years offer golden opportunities to develop the undeveloped sides of our personalities.

Scripture

Do not wear yourself out to get rich;
be wise enough to desist.

Proverbs 23:4

Prayer

O God, help my friend to see retirement
as two steps forward, not as a step
backward. Guide my friend's awareness
away from all those things that had to
be done in the past to the many things
that the future offers.

Send your Spirit to guide my friend
during this time of adjustment. Inflate
any temporary flatness with the refresh-
ing winds of freedom that retirement
brings to the golden and diamond years
of life.

Moving to a Care Center

IMAGE: BREAD CAST ON THE WATERS

Moving from a familiar place where we offered support and care to those around us to a place where we are the ones who are cared for is a transition for both body and soul. Perhaps we no longer have the physical space we once had, but the soul's space is never limited.

There can be a gracefulness in allowing ourselves to be cared for. Bread cast upon the waters can and will return to nourish us. The hospitality we once offered to visitors to our homes can now be offered to nurses, orderlies and other caregivers. More often than not, they will appreciate and reciprocate. Any room anywhere can possess its own soulfulness in proportion to the heart that beats with gratitude within it.

Scripture

Send out your bread upon the waters,
for after many days you will get it back.

Ecclesiastes 11:1

Prayer

Mary of Nazareth, you knew the pain of moving from your home. Jesus' death made it necessary for you to enter a new dwelling under the care of his beloved disciple, John. You adjusted to the stress of a different space, however. The bread of your youthful devotion—cast upon the waters at Nazareth—returned to nourish your later years.

I ask that blessing now for my loved one making a move to a care center. May it be a nourishing oasis where both guests and caregivers share hospitality and gentle kindness.

Loss of Physical Abilities

IMAGE: THE LIBERTY BELL

Perhaps the most famous bell in America is the Liberty Bell. How strange that the most renowned of all bells has a crack in it; it is not perfect. Human beings are like that renowned bell—imperfect, yet so very special!

For any number of reasons, our bodies give way to disabilities. Yet, the human heart need never experience limitations. Its freedom is eternal.

Scripture

"For the eyes of the Lord are on the
    righteous,
    and his ears are open to their prayer."

1 Peter 3:12

Prayer

O God, you sent your Son, Jesus, to
restore the body and renew the soul. He
opened the eyes and ears of people and
healed their bodies, so that they might
receive the good news of the gospel. On
his cross, he understood firsthand the
pain of lost physical abilities.

Help my friend to be patient with any
physical limitations and to treasure your
promise of eternal life. Bring the healing
that leaves the human heart ever free of
any limitations the body might experience.

Relinquishing a Driver's License

IMAGE: HOLDING THE REINS OF A CHARIOT

The "chariot!" Young people dream of the day they will be licensed to drive. To get behind the wheel is to harness a whirlwind of mobility, to go where legs could never carry! Thus, to relinquish the wheel after a lifetime of driving is to let go of the reins, to release the dream of certain freedoms.

Laughter can help us with the pain of loss. The story is told of two hospital sisters running out of gas on a rural road in Alabama. They decided they would have to hike to a filling station half a mile away, but what would they use for a gasoline container? When they looked in their trunk, they found a bedpan. So they walked to the station, filled the pan with gas, walked back to their car, and started to pour the contents of the bedpan into their gas tank.

Just then, a preacher and his wife drove by. He did a double take, looked at his wife, and said, "Now, Honey, there's faith!"

Scripture

As they continued walking and talking, a chariot of fire and horses of fire separated the two of them, and Elijah ascended in a whirlwind into heaven.

2 Kings 2:11

Prayer

To slow down, to stop, to let go of the wheel, goes against the grain. It is like the parting of Elisha and Elijah—the chariot departs and Elisha is left to walk.

Great God, the source of whirlwinds, spinning wheels, and all moving things, be with my friend in the winding down and halting moments of life. Let my friend surrender gracefully the passports of former days—titles to autos and licenses to drive. Turn my friend's journey—by foot, cane, walker, or wheelchair—in your direction, never to lose faith in your constant presence.

Depending on Medicaid

IMAGE: THE AMERICAN FLAG

It was grandparents' visiting day at school. As the children recited the Pledge of Allegiance, one smiling grandchild faced his grandparents instead of the flag. Later, when Grandpa suggested that the child should have faced the Stars and Stripes, the symbol of our homeland, the child responded, "But Grandpa, you and Grandma are homeland to me!"

True enough. We, the people, are the nation—the homeland. To care for the nation is to care for one another. People should not regret that they are cared for by their homeland, for we are "one nation, under God, indivisible, with liberty and justice for all."

Scripture

The spirit of the Lord God is upon me,
because the Lord has anointed me;
he has sent me to bring good news to the
    oppressed,
to bind up the brokenhearted,
to proclaim liberty to the captives.

Isaiah 61:1

Prayer

God bless America, a land that cares for
its people. Help my loved one realize that
all of us, young and old, are the nation
and that the care our nation shows to its
own is what makes our homeland just
and compassionate. May my loved one
accept Medicaid with grace and gratitude, not with humility and shame. May
my loved one understand that receiving
aid and comfort neither depletes our
nation nor diminishes the individual in
any way; rather, it makes all of us
strong.

Hospitalization

IMAGE: A SAINT BERNARD DOG

Consider the famous Saint Bernard dog, bred to rescue marooned travelers on the frozen mountain passes of Switzerland. When we think of dear ones hospitalized, we want to be like a Saint Bernard: warm-hearted, exuberant, our presence bringing a smile. How great it is to bring relief and rest to those we care about who are hospitalized.

Hospitals are not really good places in which to find rest. Patients are so often probed, poked, and awakened in the middle of the night with, "Are you awake?" Perhaps our prayers from afar are just what the doctor ordered!

Scripture

The centurion answered, "Lord, I am not worthy to have you come under my roof; but only speak the word, and my servant will be healed."

Matthew 8:8

Prayer

O Lord, there is power in the word. Just as your words to the centurion leapt across time and space to heal his servant, may the very real power of my prayer enter into my friend's hospital room bringing that peace which supports healing.

O Lord, speak again your word. Bless the healing skills of all the doctors and nurses so that your servant, my friend, may be healed.

A Life-Threatening Illness

IMAGE: A KITE SAILING IN A SPRING WIND

Spring! A time of zephyrean breezes, budding trees, and kites scudding through the sky. Fickle winds lift these colorful salutes to spring, only to dip them, drop them, and lift them again. Such is the flight path of life itself.

Perhaps angels are the kites of heaven—climbing, dipping, soaring, lifting our spirits when we are too weak to fly.

Scripture

I am going to send an angel in front of you, to guard you on the way and to bring you to the place that I have prepared.

Exodus 23:20

Prayer

"Angels of God, guardians dear, to whom God's love commits us here, ever this day be at our side, to light and guard, to rule and guide." Be with my friend in weak moments. Uphold my friend's spirit when it is too weak to fly.

In the "Pits"

IMAGE: PITS AT THE RACE TRACK

At the Indianapolis 500 auto race, the machines rally and roar. They zig, zag, and accelerate, trying to reach and exceed the current records. How like our society this is: speeding up with greater and greater demands for success, lots of pressure to go further, be greater, accomplish more!

On the racetrack, sooner or later each driver slows down to cruise into the pits, where tires are changed, oil is checked, engine is tuned, driver is coached—all accomplished in record time.

Similarly, we all need our moments in the "pits"—down time, sad time, grieving time, moody time, renewing time. We cannot keep the racetrack pace without receiving the same attention as racing machines. We need fresh tread on our spirit, the oil of human kindness, the tune of stillness, and the soulful coaching of prayer.

Scripture

May the God of hope fill you with all joy and peace in believing, so that you may abound in hope by the power of the Holy Spirit.

Romans 15:13

Prayer

Help my dear friend, O God, to see the "pits" as a time to grow, reassess, and feed the soul. The darkness there leads to the light of renewal, for creativity brews in the quiet dark of the imagination. Spirit of Hope, help my friend hold on until you bring something new and good out of the "pits."

Hospice

IMAGE: A REST STOP FOR PILGRIMS

Hospice is a place of shelter for pilgrims. It is an oasis of rest, a home away from home. All of us are pilgrims on the journey of life, and all of us need the sustaining hospitality of others along our pilgrim paths.

Perhaps the first hospice occurred when the angels came to Jesus in the wilderness and gave him comfort and nourishment. As members of the very body of Jesus, we can expect the same soothing ministrations of angels.

Scripture

And the Spirit immediately drove him out into the wilderness. He was in the wilderness forty days, tempted by Satan; and he was with the wild beasts; and the angels waited on him.

Mark 1:12-13

Prayer

I thank you, Lord, that there is a room— a hospice full of love and care—for my friend. Send your holy angels from heaven to minister with your peace. May these holy spirits sustain and lift up the spirit of my loved one.

Home Confinement

IMAGE: "SAFE AT HOME!"

Sometimes the baseball runner slides into home plate in a cloud of dust. The umpire, eyes alert, arms sweeping wide, declares the runner "Safe!"

Sometimes, on our journey around the bases of daily living, we have to "hit the dirt" and "slide into home." Perhaps we're confined at home, especially if we're ill or fatigued. "Safe at home" is a good place to be.

Scripture

Now Simon's mother-in-law was in bed
with a fever, and they told him about her
at once. He came and took her by the
hand and lifted her up. Then the fever
left her, and she began to serve them.

Mark 1:30-31

Prayer

Bless my friend's home, O Lord. Just as
you went to Peter's home and to the
home of your good friend, Lazarus, be a
guest in the home of my friend. Fill it
with the energy of rest and healing that
is so needed at this time.

Loss in a Natural Disaster

IMAGE: THE SEEDLINGS OF YELLOWSTONE

Near the end of the twentieth century, fires raged through vast areas of Yellowstone Park leaving blackened stumps jutting above heaps of ash. The scene resembled a moonscape: no life to be seen anywhere. So often, after a natural disaster, nature's signature upon the earth seems to say, "No life shall return here." But this is an illusion.

Within a year, tiny green seedlings peeked up out of the ashes of their parents and ancestors throughout those vast areas of Yellowstone Park. These were the new trees that will grow to full maturity in the new century. Like the Phoenix rising from the ashes, these delicate green shoots are signals of new life emerging from chaos.

Scripture

In the beginning when God created the heavens and the earth, the earth was a formless void and darkness covered the face of the deep.

Genesis 1:1-2

Prayer

O God, I mourn the chaos that, without warning, has destroyed my friends' treasures that money cannot replace. Like the seedlings of Yellowstone that grew out of the ashes of catastrophe, may new hope arise beyond the shock of this moment.

I now stand together in prayer with those I love who have lost so much. I weave my spirit with theirs until that day when their faith and hope are rewarded with a peaceful letting go, a gradual healing, and a newness of all that is truly priceless.

Family Alienation or Separation

IMAGE: A TOWER

The headline announced, "High Wire Rescue!" Ten-year-old John had climbed to the top of a 120-foot utility tower whose cables hummed with high-voltage electricity. Although his sixteen-year-old brother attempted to rescue John, neither boy was able to move from that height until a trained rescue squad brought them down safely to the welcome arms of their waiting parents.

At one time or another, all families suffer the tower of silence and alienation as a result of anger, hurt feelings, misunderstandings. At the top of the tower, clinging to pride and fear, family members remain separated from those they love, not knowing how to get down and reconnect.

So often, a simple plea for reunion and reconciliation, as well as an admission of some personal responsibility for the separation, is all it takes to reunite families.

Scripture

When Jesus came to the place, he looked up and said to him, "Zacchaeus, hurry and come down; for I must stay at your house today."

Luke 19:5

Prayer

Dear Lord, the further up a tower we go, the harder it is to get down. We don't know what to say or what to do.

Jesus, you told Zacchaeus to hurry and come down, "for I must stay at your house today." Call my friends down from their towers of separation and alienation. Stay in the homes of their hearts as they long for reunion. Please bring them together again in your own time.

Criminal Assault or Abuse

IMAGE: A PEARL NESTLED IN A SHELL

Over the years, the love and affirmation people receive from their family and friends build a protective shell around the pearl of their inner core—their personhood. But when criminal assault or abuse of any kind wounds them, they feel that protective shell around their inner core has been cracked. But it need not crumble. Victor Frankl, a Jewish psychiatrist who survived Hitler's concentration camps, wrote that it was possible for even the most abused inmates to retain their integrity in the face of the most unjust and demeaning treatment.

How distressing that anyone, in any way, would wreak violence upon the body or spirit of another human being. When that does happen, those of us who know the victim feel anger, rage, and deep concern, for a part of our own personhood has been violated as well. We feel the wounds personally, because we know that we are connected to others through the love we share.

Scripture

Blessed be the God and Father of our Lord Jesus Christ, the Father of mercies and the God of all consolation, who consoles us in all our affliction, so that we may be able to console those who are in any affliction with the consolation with which we ourselves are consoled by God.

2 Corinthians 1:3-4

Prayer

As recovery gradually takes place after this outrage, O God, surround my friend's wounds with this garland of prayer. Only your Son, wounded on the cross, can bring the deep and lasting healing that is needed at this time. For this, I pray.

Burglary or Vandalism

IMAGE: A FRIENDLY FIRE IN A FIREPLACE

In Greek mythology, Prometheus lit his torch from the sun and gave the gift of fire to humankind as an everlasting gift. Ever after, the fire of the hearth would be the source of energy and warmth for every home. No wonder hearth and heart are related words.

When burglars or vandals violate the sacred spaces of our homes, they trample our hearts as well, for our hearts abide within our homes. What is taken or damaged goes far deeper than our material possessions.

Scripture

You shall not steal.
Exodus 20:15

Prayer

Holy Spirit, Flame of Love, hover over my friends' despoiled home. Consecrate it once more, for those who dwell therein are a beloved family of God. Bless their hearth and lift up their saddened, frightened, angry hearts.

Loss of a Pet

IMAGE: THE PANDA

An ancient legend tells of pure white bears who observed the murder of a friendly shepherd and grieved the burning of the shepherd's hut. In sorrow, the bears blackened their arms and legs with the ashes of the shepherd's dwelling and rubbed their eyes and ears with the soot. Ever after, the fur on their descendants carries the black marks of the Pandas' long-ago mourning.

Scripture

The cow and the bear shall graze,
    their young shall lie down together;
    and the lion shall eat straw like the ox.
                                        Isaiah 11:7

Prayer

Generous Creator, there was a friendship between pet and master that will
linger for years to come. Console my
friend in the loss of a dear companion.
May the void left behind be made more
gentle by memories of happy times.

Downsizing

IMAGE: THE PARING KNIFE

Cutting, slashing, paring: all words with an unpleasant ring to them. The same is true with "downsizing." Might the corporate knife that downsizes be a dagger that eventually cuts to the bone of the human spirit, thus diminishing the life force of the corporate body? One wonders. Time will tell, but in the meantime, company loyalty is slashed and wonderful employees are cast adrift.

Scripture

My soul languishes for your salvation;
I hope in your word.

Psalm 119:81

Prayer

O Lord, it seems that loyal service and work are being "downsized" these days. Help my friend realize that the slashing knives that sever employment can wound our security but cannot touch our souls.

May my friend's search for a new opportunity be Spirit-led, and may it turn what is loss into gain, what is darkness into light.

Bankruptcy

IMAGE: THE CLAM DIGGER

Onlookers watched him as he stood knee-deep in the ocean tide, the waves rippling and bubbling around him. Over and over he poked his hooked pole into the soggy sand, and each time he came up empty-handed. Finally, he hitched up his britches against the lapping waters and moved on to a new spot, a new hope. Losing interest in the persistent clam digger, the onlookers, too, moved on. Then came a cry of delight that echoed along the shoreline for all to hear. From the surging tide, out of the flotsam, the man held up the object of his desire: a large clam.

Scripture

Then Job arose, tore his robe, shaved his head, and fell on the ground and worshiped. He said, "Naked I came from my mother's womb, and naked shall I return there; the Lord gave, and the Lord has taken away; blessed be the name of the Lord."

Job 1:20-21

Prayer

O God, my friend has waded through the surging tides of fortune and misfortune and has come up empty-handed. This feels like failure, after giving such diligent effort to the cause. Let my friend humbly and gracefully face the end of these efforts and move on, for yesterday is done and today leans toward tomorrow. Stir new dreams in my friend. May today's sense of emptiness, loss and failure be replaced by the fullness of hope for better days and successful quests.

Lawsuit

IMAGE: MUSIC IN A HOLLOW PLACE

Edging the perimeters of a desert city is a path for walking and bicycling. At several points around the city the path drops below ground and becomes a tunnel, leaving the noise and bustle of the city far above.

He was there in one of the tunnels, seated in a chair, a music stand in front of him. Oblivious to traffic overhead and joggers passing by, he sat there every morning playing his saxophone. Was he exiled from a condo? Was he threatened with a lawsuit for violating a noise ordinance? He never said. He just created music in that hollow place.

Scripture

When any of you has a grievance against another, do you dare to take it to court before the unrighteous, instead of taking it before the saints?

1 Corinthians 6:1

Prayer

O Great Judge of Hearts and Minds, hear the prayers of my friend who is suffering the frustrations and fears of an unnecessary lawsuit. Grant my friend the grace of endurance and forbearance, for in the end all things will be righted on your scale. During this time, fill hollow hearts with music that sings of hope and justice.

Losing the Big Game

IMAGE: WINNING AND LOSING

In 1995 the Nebraska football team was the best in the land. Early in the season, they crushed the out-manned Arizona State Sun Devils. On January 1, 1996, the Big Red machine won its second straight national championship by beating Florida in the Fiesta Bowl in Tempe, Arizona.

In the fall of the same year, Nebraska returned to Tempe to play Arizona State again. Before a stunned crowd, virtually the same Arizona State team that had been humiliated by Nebraska the year before upset the Huskers, holding them scoreless.

The unheralded Sun Devils went on to a Cinderella-like undefeated season and a chance to play for the national championship themselves. In the Rose Bowl, however, their dream of a national title was snatched away in the last minute by an Ohio State touchdown pass.

The Sun Devils had played their best. There was reason for tears, but no shame. The wisdom gained from a loss is to grow stronger in broken places, for where the fractured bone mends becomes the strongest point!

Scripture

Do not boast about tomorrow,
   for you do not know what a day
   may bring.

Proverbs 27:1

Prayer

I give thanks to you, O God, for the
exciting memories my friend holds of
past victories. If so much had not been
ventured, it would not be so hard to
lose. But sports would be boring if good
teams only tied. There is reason for my
friend's grief but none for shame. Grant,
O God, that my friend holds dear the
good memories and rejoices in your love
for all of us, a love that makes us all
winners when it counts.

Part 2:
Losses through Death

"Blessed are those who mourn,
for they will be comforted."
Matthew 5:4

The Death of a Neighbor

IMAGE: THE FAMOUS BOYS' TOWN STATUE

This is the endearing image of a boy carrying a smaller boy over his shoulder, with the caption, "He ain't heavy, Father. He's my brother."

He ain't heavy, he's my brother.

She ain't heavy, she's my sister.

He ain't heavy, he's my neighbor.

She ain't heavy, she's my neighbor.

Scripture

"And who is my neighbor?" Jesus replied, "A man was going down from Jerusalem to Jericho, and fell into the hands of robbers."

Luke 10:29-30

Prayer for the Deceased

Our friend was such a good neighbor, O God. Warm exchanges across the years often lightened the burdens of long days. May all your saints come to welcome our neighbor to a realm of peace, joy and contentment.

Prayer for Those Who Mourn

Bring solace to a grieving neighborhood, O God, as hearts heavy with grief still hear our neighbor's friendly voice. May they remember that the warmth and friendship of this good person will never be gone.

The Death of a Co-Worker

IMAGE: AN EMPTY WHEELBARROW

Were you to visit a farm or factory or office
in Ireland, upon leaving you would bid fare-
well by saying, "And God bless the work!"
and the worker would respond, "And bless
you, too!"

Mellow twilight time,

the barrow stands still.

Word processors shut down.

The Dow is closed.

Doors are locked.

Day is done.

Then comes this day

which is the last work

for our treasured co-worker.

God has blessed the work

and through our colleague's presence

blessed us, too!

Scripture

"When evening came, the owner of the vineyard said to his manager, 'Call the laborers and give them their pay.'"

Matthew 20:8

Prayer for the Deceased

Day's work is now well done, O God. We pray for the rest and reward of our co-worker, after the labors of a lifetime.

Prayer for Those Who Mourn

We give thanks to you, O God, for the privilege of having shared in the labors and companionship of our co-worker. Console our colleague's loved ones and family as we share in their loss.

The Death of a Beloved Life Partner

IMAGE: THE SEA

Like Peter leaping into the sea, sweethearts
let go and fall into the sea of love—there to
find their treasure.

Falling in love,

letting go, deep waters.

A blessed voyage

upon the sea of life.

This sweetheart's love,

great energy surging,

a strong current,

deep and ever constant.

Now another letting go

until God rejoins—

a future time,

a distant shore.

Scripture

When Simon Peter heard that it was the Lord, he put on some clothes, for he was naked, and jumped into the sea.

John 21:7

Prayer for the Deceased

May this beloved one enter your welcoming embrace, Lord. Thanks be to you for a voyage of love shared so unconditionally.

Prayer for Those Who Mourn

Jesus, come across the turbulent waters of grief to embrace and uphold my friend's heart, broken with loss. Grant solace, comfort and hope; bring healing and peace.

The Death of a Parent

IMAGE: THE FLIGHT OF THE EAGLE

A good parent is like an eagle watching over
its young with keen eyes—so happy when
the young learn to fly.

We remember

a loving parent

filled with joy

when eaglets learned to fly.

Now that strength is gone,

this good spirit soars

beyond earth's rim

toward the morning star.

Scripture

But those who wait for the Lord shall
    renew their strength,
  they shall mount up with wings like
    eagles,
they shall run and not be weary,
  they shall walk and not faint.

Isaiah 40:31

Prayer for the Deceased

God of All Mercies, lift this good father
(or mother) on eagles' wings beyond all
earthly cares. From your heavenly reign,
may this loving parent watch over the
eaglets of all generations.

Prayer for Those Who Mourn

Dear Jesus, you compared yourself to a
parent bird. Gather now this grieving
family under your wings of solace. Let
them know the uplifting release of your
peace.

The Death of an Elderly Person

IMAGE: THE HOLY MOUNTAINS OF OUR FAITH

Mountains—white-haired, craggy oldsters—
tower above the plains. These old peaks can
be fitting images for our beloved elders who
have endured and held steady through the
years. For so long, their life provided a horizon and a frame for our younger lives.

Holy mountain
Moses—revealing
Jesus—ascending
path to life unending.

White-cragged mountain
youth—arising
now old—vaulting
up to the heavens.

Mountain summits
for ages—growing
now—glowing
all seen clearly now.

Scripture

And he will destroy on this mountain
    the shroud that is cast over all peoples,
    the sheet that is spread over all nations;
    he will swallow up death forever.
Isaiah 25:7

Prayer for the Deceased

Our dear one is like some beloved old
mountain, O God, white-topped, face-
lined, and chipped with all the years.
With your hand now resting upon the
sacred crown of our friend's soul, grant
the blessing of eternal life.

Prayer for Those Who Mourn

You give your mountains at sunset, O
God, a mellow color called alpenglow.
May my friends who grieve the loss of
their beloved reflect that alpenglow in
the memories of their loved one—a life
well lived and living still in sweet memories.

The Death of a Guardian of Our Welfare

IMAGE: THE GUARDIANS' BADGE OR INSIGNIA

When a policeman was gunned down by an assault rifle in the hands of a young gang member, his sister recalled how as children she and her brother played a game called "I Touched You Last!" In fact, she recalled, they even played that game as adults, playfully tapping each other on the shoulders as they would part. Then the woman exclaimed, "In a beautiful way, he has touched us all last."

Protector's shield,

badge of valor,

emblem of service,

touch us last!

Accepted, treasured,

pinned upon the heart,

worn with pride,

touch us last!

This brave comrade,

guardian in harms way,

bearer of courage,

touch us last!

Scripture

Our soul waits for the Lord;
he is our help and shield.

Psalm 33:20

Prayer for the Deceased

O Lord, we pray for our departed guardian. Send Michael the Archangel to be an escort through the heavenly gates, where there are no more tears, no more conflicts—only peace, joy and eternal safety.

Prayer for Those Who Mourn

We give thanks, Lord, for the courage of our guardian's heart, and we grieve with the family and friends of this brave soul. Be present to all of us. Bring us peace.

The Death of a Person Suffering with AIDS

IMAGE: THE AIDS QUILT

When we think of quilts, we think of generations coming together in a multicolored composite of patches, providing warmth down through the years. Some quilts are even called "comforters."

Is our journey toward the kingdom of God

like the making of a quilt,

piecing the patches together as we go?

For some, the last piece in the quilt

is the patch of suffering

and their badge of courage.

The ugly patch called AIDS,

when turned over by love,

is the color of hope.

Scripture

And all of you must clothe yourselves with humility in your dealings with one another, for
"God opposes the proud,
but gives grace to the humble."

Prayer for the Deceased

O Lord, the white pall over the casket is the last patch in the AIDS quilt—now folded up in faith. We pray that the pattern of this life and its suffering will also be folded up in your welcoming arms.

Prayer for Those Who Mourn

Renew us, Lord, as we mourn this tragic death. May the family and friends of this beautiful soul stitch together the hope of your consoling promise for a better life beyond all afflictions.

The Death of a Person Suffering with Alzheimer's

IMAGE: THE CELTIC CROSS

Ireland is filled with unique stone crosses whose crossbeams are intersected by a stone circle. People suffering Alzheimer's often walk around in a circle—one of the mysterious side effects of this disease. As the disease progresses, of course, the circle of awareness for those who suffer becomes a tighter and more restrictive bond.

Life comes full circle.
Quiet in the womb,
we come forth crying,
learn to talk and understand,
and someday say wondrous words,
like "Thanks be to God!"
and "I love you!"
In later years, a silent foe
creeps in, shuts out memory,
silences speech, erects a wall.
Now death has intervened.
And Christ himself, once walled in,
at the center of the circle,
sets our loved one free!

Scripture

So they took away the stone. And Jesus looked upward and said, "Father, I thank you for having heard me. I knew that you always hear me, but I have said this for the sake of the crowd standing here, so that they may believe that you sent me." When he had said this, he cried with a loud voice, "Lazarus, come out!"

John 11:41-43

Prayer for the Deceased

Jesus, you entered into stony tombs to bring resurrection and new life. Now, in your mercy, call forth the spirit of our friend previously walled in by Alzheimer's. May your peaceful reign open wide with welcome, and may those sweet but forgotten memories return.

Prayer for Those Who Mourn

Bless those who mourn the loss of this beautiful person, O God. Let memories of a vibrant life, before Alzheimer's, be gentle and consoling. Let this grief look toward a freedom far beyond the restraints of disease.

The Death of a Person Suffering with Cancer

IMAGE: FLANDERS FIELDS

Poet John McCrea immortalized Flanders Fields, filled with white crosses and wind-blown poppies. Beneath those crosses lie the remains of heroes slain in fierce battles. This vivid image does not let us forget those brave warriors.

But there are other tests of endurance not fought on battlefields, other brave warriors who fight life-and-death struggles. Cancer is a merciless and aggressive invader. Even when its legions sound retreat following chemotherapy or radiation, they have been known to attack another day. Now the cancer battle is over; it is now a time for peace.

Those who lost brave battles
will rise to win the war,
and death itself be vanquished
and tears shall be no more.

Scripture

I have fought the good fight, I have
finished the race, I have kept the faith.
From now on there is reserved for me
the crown of righteousness.

2 Timothy 4:7-8

Prayer for the Deceased

O Jesus, the malignant enemy, cancer,
has finally overcome all the defenses of
medicine and care, but not the human
spirit of our friend. May this brave soul
now feast at the victory banquet of
heaven.

Prayer for Those Who Mourn

Bless those who grieve the loss of their
loved one, O God. May they come to
know the peace that puts an end to
every war.

The Death of a Person Suffering with Heart Disease

IMAGE: THE HEART OF JESUS

Jesus' heart was filled with compassion and overflowed with love. It was pierced by the lance—broken but never conquered. As it embraced Mary of Magdala in the garden of her grief, it embraces all of us as we face the mystery of death.

We recall the heartbeats of a lifetime

cut short by death:

a heart that loved family and friends;

a heart that did a lifetime of work;

a heart that beat with compassion;

a heart, worn out

from loving

and living,

now still.

Scripture

"For where your treasure is, there your heart will be also."

Luke 12:34

Prayer for the Deceased

Saint Augustine said that our hearts are restless until they rest in you, O God. May the loving heart of our friend, now stilled, possess all the treasures of heaven.

Prayer for Those Who Mourn

The loss of a loved one leaves dismay and numbness in its wake. Pour your love, Brother Jesus, into the hearts that grieve. Embrace them, as you once embraced the heart of grief-stricken Mary of Magdala.

The Death of a Person Who Suffered a Stroke

IMAGE: THE ALBATROSS

Coleridge's *The Rime of the Ancient Mariner*
presents the image of an albatross falling off
the neck of the mariner at the moment of
prayer—thus setting him free.

Monitors, tubes, machines:

our modern way of saying

"Life is precious,

support life!"

Yet, there comes a point in time,

on the way to new life,

when these machines

become bonds that restrain.

They are cast away now,

like the albatross,

and newfound freedom

opens the way to everlasting life.

Scripture

"Very truly, I tell you, when you were younger, you used to fasten your own belt and to go wherever you wished. But when you grow old, you will stretch out your hands, and someone else will fasten a belt around you and take you where you do not wish to go."

John 21:18

Prayer for the Deceased

The stroke's grip, like a tight vise, no longer binds the soul of our friend, God of Mercy. May death's release now bring to this soul your freedom and peace.

Prayer for Those Who Mourn

O God of Hope, may the image of their loved one, now finally unbound, comfort those who mourn. May they find consolation in your promise of new life beyond earthly bonds and cares.

Great Pain Ending in Death

IMAGE: THE CUP OF WINE AT THE LAST SUPPER

When Jesus' disciples asked about their place in his kingdom, he told them that they didn't know what they were asking: "Are you able to drink the cup that I drink?" (Mark 10:38) Jesus knew that his cup was full of pain and sorrow and that he would drink it to the dregs. All humankind is familiar with this cup.

This pain now ended—

this cup now emptied—

shall now be filled

at heaven's banquet.

Once more the best of wine

has been saved for last.

Scripture

Then he took a cup, and after giving thanks he gave it to them, saying, "Drink from it, all of you; for this is my blood of the covenant, which is poured out for many for the forgiveness of sins. I tell you, I will never again drink of this fruit of the vine until that day when I drink it new with you in my Father's kingdom."

Matthew 26:27-29

Prayer for the Deceased

For the life of our friend now emptied by the pain of dying, O God, we ask for a better time, a painless place where the fullness of your joy shall overflow.

Prayer for Those Who Mourn

We journey with those who suffer this noble pain of grief, O God. As they let go of their loved one, may their stress subside and their hope abound.

A Sudden Death

IMAGE: MAKING PLANS FOR TOMORROW

People plan today for tomorrow. It sometimes happens, however, that when tomorrow arrives, the plans matter little. "One
moment, talking about tomorrow, and the
next moment, gone. It is so sudden."

A friend sat down to plan a banquet,

and the next moment the friend was gone!

Snatched away by the angels

to another invitation, another table.

We all expect tomorrow and plan ahead.

We often plan for holiday feasts.

But for all there must be a last meal,

a last chapter in the book of life.

But friends and loved ones

who have served us at the table of care,

who have broken the bread of kindness

shall not thirst nor hunger at heaven's table.

Scripture

"Be dressed for action and have your lamps lit; be like those who are waiting for their master to return from the wedding banquet."

Luke 12:35-36

Prayer for the Deceased

We thirst for the milk of human kindness, O God. May this good person, who quenched that hunger for others, now be fed at your eternal banquet.

Prayer for Those Who Mourn

The sudden loss of one who was "always there" always leaves a void. We stand in solidarity with our good friends who mourn, O God. May your angels fold wings of peace over their troubled hearts.

A Violent Death

IMAGE: A SWORD OR LANCE

While Mary stood at the foot of the cross in
the wind and rain, a cruel and violent thrust
of the lance pierced the side of her beloved
Son: "...and a sword will pierce your own
soul too" (Luke 2:35).

Who closer to Jesus
than another victim of violence?
Jesus walked that path.
He knows life's sudden end.

And Mary, source of his life,
traumatized and anguished,
stood by his cross
at death's cruel thrust.

Simeon's prophecy now fulfilled—
a sword of sorrow
a cry of anguish
on Calvary's awful hill.

But Mary waited,
as we all must wait,
at a stone-closed tomb
until Easter hope pierces our pain.

Scripture

And the child's father and mother were amazed at what was being said about him. Then Simeon blessed them and said to his mother Mary, "This child is destined for the falling and the rising of many in Israel, and to be a sign that will be opposed so that the inner thoughts of many will be revealed—and a sword will pierce your own soul too."

Luke 2:33-35

Prayer for the Deceased

May your angels, O God, be quick to offer safe passage for your faithful servant beyond this earthly tragedy into a realm of peace and joy. May they escort this dear soul into your eternal rest.

Prayer for Those Who Mourn

May the sword-pierced and mourning hearts of our grief-stricken friends take comfort, O God, with the sorrowful mother of your Son. She waited for Resurrection—as we must all wait.

The Death of a Person by Suicide

IMAGE: A BOAT TOSSED UPON ROUGH SEAS

No matter how firm the rigging or deep the hull, a ship sometimes becomes a fragile vessel amid raging storms.

We survive in a vale of tears,
beneath a cloud of uncertainty.
"Whys" and "if onlys" give us no rest.

Yet, in our searching we find certitude.
The ending of this precious life was not right
for this beloved, and was not right for us.

When our boat seems so small,
the waves so large, we must find
a better port than this.

For this loved one, the enemy Death
poured through. But it is not for us
to judge defenses that did not hold.

And what of God?
Our Creator is surely strong enough
to pick up the pieces of self-ended lives.

Will our God,
who marks the sparrow's course,
judge life by one moment of ending
or by the rowings of a lifetime?

Scripture

And while they were sailing he fell asleep. A windstorm swept down on the lake, and the boat was filling with water, and they were in danger. They went to him and woke him up, shouting, "Master, Master, we are perishing!" And he woke up and rebuked the wind and the raging waves; they ceased, and there was a calm.

Luke 8:23-24

Prayer for the Deceased

The turbulent waves have ceased, O God. Bring our dear journeyer to a tranquil shore. May an eternal tide of peace wash over this troubled traveler's soul.

Prayer for Those Who Mourn

In this time of confusion, mourning, and "if onlys," O God, unbind the grief-stricken hearts of my friends with your grace. May your Spirit, the Consoler, calm the tempest in their wondering hearts and reassure them of your unconditional love.

A Miscarriage

IMAGE: A CLOUD THAT BLOCKS THE DAWN

When the cresting sun is blocked by the shadow of clouds, the world seems shrouded in a light that is not fully light.

Sometimes clouds cover dawn.

Where light was to be—is not.

Where life would appear—does not.

So we wait for a new day.

Sorrow is our night.

New hope must be our morning.

Scripture

"Are not five sparrows sold for two pennies? Yet not one of them is forgotten in God's sight."

Luke 12:6

Prayer for the Tiniest of Creatures

You know the place of the tiniest sparrow, O God, so surely you know where there is the beginning of life. Your sight is great enough to see and take to your heart the tiniest of souls.

Prayer for Those Who Mourn

O God, may this cloud of sadness that obscures an expected life fade with the dawning of better days and renewed hopes for my dear friends. May those who mourn find peace in your promise of abundant life.

A Stillbirth

IMAGE: JESUS IMAGED AS A MOTHER

The medieval mystic Julian of Norwich
called Jesus a true mother—in whose womb
each of us is always carried.

We want our lives to count.
So what of this life stillborn?

If to count means to call forth love,
to elicit compassion, to be missed,
then by all earthly reckoning
this child counts!

But there is another measure
that counts this life as love.

The Good Shepherd counts his sheep,
and the old ones flock through his gate;
but only the tiniest ones, the lambs,
are carried in his arms.

Scripture

"I am the good shepherd. I know my own and my own know me."

John 10:14

Prayer for the Deceased

We entrust this dear child to you, O God, knowing the limitless expanse of your arms and the unfathomable depth of your heart. This child, your child, returns to nestle in your care.

Prayer for Those Who Mourn

The great disappointments of life can only be redeemed in your time, O God, and in your house. Hold against your breast my friends who mourn. Let them cling to your promise of eternal life. Console them.

The Death of an Infant

IMAGE: A CRADLE IN THE NURSERY OF HEAVEN

If heaven is a place secure, a home of joyful
sounds, then surely an infant's cry is welcome there!

When sudden death comes
like a thief in the night,
we are left with anger and fear,
numbness and grief.

Like the first Christmas families,
mourning the innocents,
so beautiful the gift,
so great the loss.

Like children who led the Lord
on the Sunday of palms,
holy innocents go before,
wait for us at heaven's door.

Scripture

"Have you never read,
    'Out of the mouths of infants
    and nursing babies
    you have prepared praise
    for yourself'?"

Matthew 21:16

Prayer for the Deceased

All your Holy Innocents, O God, come to meet this beautiful child of our dear friends. Lead the way to the cradle of our Savior's arms and his lullaby of love.

Prayer for Those Who Mourn

Comfort the hearts of our friends that bear the pain of this death, O God. May the eyes of their souls gaze upon the safety and peace of heaven's nursery until that day of joyful reunion in your kingdom of everlasting life.

The Death of a Toddler

IMAGE: THE SKIPPING CHILD

Perhaps the oldest dances in the world are
those of the frolicking colt, the leaping lamb,
the skipping child.

On our earthly journey,
adults lead children out of play
into work.

On our heavenly journey,
might children lead adults out of work
into play?

If our only value were work,
then a child's loss
is total loss.

But if playfulness is valuable,
are not children at home
in heaven?

When the kingdom comes,
will we be led in
by skipping and laughing children?

Scripture

Then little children were being brought to him in order that he might lay his hands on them and pray. The disciples spoke sternly to those who brought them; but Jesus said, "Let the little children come to me, and do not stop them; for it is to such as these that the kingdom of heaven belongs." And he laid his hands on them and went on his way.

Matthew 19:13-15

Prayer for the Deceased

May this dear child of our friends, a sweet beloved of yours, Lord, skip toward your waiting arms. May this child find eternal delight in the playground of your love.

Prayer for Those Who Mourn

We stand with our friends who mourn, O God, in this valley of tears. Support their aching hearts. Make gentle their healing. Let their hearts skip with joy at the sweet memories of this young life.

The Death of a Young Boy

IMAGE: THE SPRING WINDS

The spring winds herald a season of promise. They tease new buds and lift the human spirit out of winter's dormant rest. The spring wind is so much like the effervescence and energies of the young boy.

Jesus was once a young boy.
He ran with the wind
and dreamed youth's dreams:
the hero's quest,
the search for the pearl,
the contest,
the victor's thrill.

He is Alpha-Omega,
Lord of the universe,
the Incarnate Word,
yet he never knew
long adulthood—
cut short by the cross
thrust into life's path.

Scripture

"I am the Alpha and the Omega," says the Lord God, who is and who was and who is to come, the Almighty.

Revelation 1:8

Prayer for the Deceased

We entrust the dear, young son of our friends to you, Jesus, as you were once his age and ran with the wind. You will understand all his dreams and give to him more than we could ever imagine.

Prayer for Those Who Mourn

A great energy has been lost, O God. Into the world of our friends who bear this cutting grief, pour your consoling grace and the strength to go on.

The Death of a Young Girl

IMAGE: A TELESCOPE

The magic eye of a telescope enables the
human eye to glimpse a distant view of
beauty not to be seen at close range. Such
are the eyes of a young girl peering into the
wonder of the universe, exclaiming with
"ooh" and "aah."

The blessed trust of little girls

dwells in the wonder years

of "oohs" and "aahs."

The blessed trust of little girls

knows Dad and Mom—

and God up close—as love.

Scripture

But Jesus called for them and said, "Let the little children come to me, and do not stop them; for it is to such as these that the kingdom of God belongs."

Luke 18:16

Prayer for the Deceased

Our friends' daughter now sees the extravagant wonders of your everlasting kingdom, O God. She sees farther than we can dream. May her joy be complete and eternal.

Prayer for Those Who Mourn

Jesus, be present to our friends in this time of darkness when hearts cannot see beyond grief. Let hope remind all that their little girl now beholds the wonder of your eternal love.

The Death of a Teenage Boy

IMAGE: YOUNG RUNNERS AND BALL PLAYERS

The passion and energy of a teenage boy are
like runners leaping over hurdles with grace
and speed on their way to the finish line.
They are like the dashing ball player stealing
second base with verve and gusto.

The young runner cannot wait.
He steals the base belly down.

The exuberance of youth.
Would we have it otherwise?

And yet, there is a danger line
between sliding safe and being out.

Some die in the exuberance of youth.

The young Jesus, could not wait
for disciples to arrive.

He hurried forth from the tomb,
and now he is out ahead,
leader of all the young
who have hurried forth too soon.

And he smiles and says, "Hurry home!"

Scripture

The two were running together, but the other disciple outran Peter and reached the tomb first. He bent down to look in and saw the linen wrappings lying there, but he did not go in.

John 20:4-5

Prayer for the Deceased

Our friend's energy, O God, is of the same essence as your creative energies. May he see your welcoming smile and hear you say, "Hurry home."

Prayer for Those Who Mourn

There is now a void, O God, where energy once played. This loss here on earth is most certainly heaven's gain. Soothe our friends' aching hearts as they find their way through these energy-empty days.

The Death of a Teenage Girl

IMAGE: VESSELS FILLED WITH HOLY OILS

At baptism we receive a lighted candle; at
confirmation we are anointed with fragrant
oil. Like the maidens in the gospel story, we
await the bridegroom's coming with the oil
in our lamps feeding the flame of anticipa-
tion.

Teenage is a poem being written,
a lyric to be sung.
No other time is so specially named
as the "teenage years."

It is that transit time
from pinafore to promenade,
that time to know who we are
and who we might become.

Our friends' daughter knew
the gospel story of the maidens,
the wise and the foolish—
awaiting the bridegroom's return.

Her vessel was filled
with the oils of baptism and confirmation.
Her lamp was burning brightly
when he came.

Scripture

"The bridegroom came, and those who were ready went with him into the wedding banquet."

Matthew 25:10

Prayer for the Deceased

Our friends' daughter remains with us, O God, in the light of life she brought to us all. The oil of her fragrant goodness lingers on. There must be great rejoicing at the wedding feast of heaven as the bridegroom brings her home.

Prayer for Those Who Mourn

A lamp has gone out and the grief is dark, O God. Console the stricken hearts of our beloved friends. Let them release their daughter's light and goodness into your care.

Death of a Young Man

IMAGE: THE SHOOTING STAR

Too often, we take the stars for granted; we may not notice them for months. Then, one crystal-clear night, a shooting star blazes across the sky and captures our full attention and our sense of wonder.

One star hangs in the heavens,

another streaks across the sky,

a blaze of beauty.

Who can say which is greater—

the steady long-lived glimmer,

or the shooting star?

For the young taken all too early,

their starry path is the Christ light—

the star that never sets.

Scripture

So we have the prophetic message more
fully confirmed. You will do well to be
attentive to this as to a lamp shining in
a dark place, until the day dawns and
the morning star rises in your hearts.

2 Peter 1:19

Prayer for the Deceased

Too quick his staying—too soon his
leaving, O God. As your creation, the life
of this young man brightened the earth
and brought light to the lives of others.
Give him now a shining and lasting
place of eternal life in your glittering
heavens.

Prayer for Those Who Mourn

In this darkness, O God, take the gaze of
our friends who mourn toward the east,
"as to a lamp shining," until the first
streaks of dawn appear and the morning
star rises in their hearts. May their
darkness be made bright by the light of
your healing.

The Death of a Young Woman

IMAGE: THE SUMMER'S LONGEST DAY

Shakespeare compared the beauty of a
young woman to an eternal summer's day
which shall never fade.

When we were young

the longest day of summer

gave free reign

to all our youthful quests.

So shall it be

at the dawning of heaven—

beauty endures

and joy shall never fade.

Scripture

After the sabbath, as the first day of the
week was dawning, Mary Magdalene and
the other Mary went to see the tomb.
And suddenly there was a great earth-
quake; for an angel of the Lord, descend-
ing from heaven, came and rolled back
the stone and sat on it.

Matthew 28:1-2

Prayer for the Deceased

We commend this young woman to that
company whose summer shall not fade,
O God. May she join the beautiful
women of the gospel, first to the tomb to
witness the glories of your Resurrection.

Prayer for Those Who Mourn

The deathly grip of winter has invaded
the meadows of summer, O God. Warm
our friends who suffer the cold bite of
grief, and let this season pass—that
summer may return.

OTHER RESOURCES FOR CONSOLATION

Our Special Pages: A Collection of Poems and Essays **Written by Cancer Survivors** by the Northeast Regional Cancer Institute. Heroic first-person accounts of battling and conquering this dreaded illness. Fifty-one stories offer spiritual guidance, practical advice about treatments and side effects, and helpful tips for living with cancer. (140 pages, $12.95)

From Grief to Grace: Images for Overcoming Sadness and Loss by Helen Reichert Lambin. This unique, gentle book addresses the powerful emotions common to all experiences of grief. Each of the ten chapters suggests several images—some religious and some secular—to assist people in naming, processing and overcoming their grief. (84 pages, $8.95)

The New Day Journal: A Journey from Grief to Healing by Sr. Mauryeen O'Brien, O.P. A book offering those who have lost a loved one a structured way to work through the "tasks of grief," including accepting the reality of the loss, experiencing the pain of grief, adjusting to the new environment in which the deceased is missing, and moving on with life. (92-page workbook, $8.95)

The Death of a Husband: Reflections for a Grieving Wife by Helen Reichert Lambin. Forty-seven short, insightful reflections for a wife who has lost a husband. Deals with the anger, grief and losses of widowhood, as well as the memories, hopes and love. (128 pages, $8.95)

The Death of a Wife: Reflections for a Grieving Husband by Robert L. Vogt. A collection of poignant reflections for any husband mourning the death of his wife. Each of the thirty-one brief stories, meditations and poems considers a different facet of the grieving process. (112 pages, $8.95)

Always Precious in Our Memory: Reflections after Miscarriage, Stillbirth or Neonatal Death by Kristen Johnson Ingram. Short, heartfelt meditations combined with carefully chosen Scripture quotations that help parents, family members and friends understand the grief, regret, anger and guilt they may be feeling at the death of a baby. (94 pages, $8.95)

AVAILABLE FROM BOOKSELLERS
OR CALL 800-397-2282